MELON CULTIVATION

Novice Guide To Ultimate & Proper Planting Techniques, Care & More

URIAH SEKANI

Table of Contents

INTRODUCTORY

Growing melons is a fun and satisfying hobby since it allows you to produce your own fresh, juicy melons in the comfort of your own home. Melons are well-liked because of their sweet flavor, high water content, and refreshing nature. Watermelon, cantaloupe, honeydew, and countless other melons are just a few examples.

Here's a quick primer on melon cultivation for those who are interested:

• Choosing the proper variety is important because melons have different needs in terms of climate, light, and soil. Pick a strain that does well in the conditions it will be exposed to. For instance, watermelons prefer warmer regions, but cantaloupes may grow in a wider temperature range.

• Melons require a soil that drains well and has a high concentration of organic materials. Loosen the soil with a garden fork or tiller and remove any weeds or other unwanted materials. Increasing the soil's fertility and ability to retain water by adding compost or well-rotted manure.

• Melons can be planted from either seeds or seedlings. After all risk of frost has gone and the soil temperature has remained above 60 degrees Fahrenheit (15 degrees Celsius), seeds can be sown straight into the prepared soil. Plant seeds at a depth of about an inch, and space them out as directed by the seed packet.

• Proper maintenance includes watering melons often, especially during dry spells. Be sure to water thoroughly and often to maintain an even moisture level in the soil. However, overwatering might cause root rot, so be careful. Mulching the soil around your plants is a great way to keep the soil moist and prevent weeds from taking over.

• Watermelons and other forms of vining melons require trellises or other means of support during their growth. Keeping the fruit off the ground and away from rot can be accomplished by staking the vines. Vines can be trained to climb trellises, fences, or other structures.

• Aphids, cucumber beetles, powdery mildew, and fungal infections are just some of the pests and illnesses that can affect melons. Keep an eye out for any symptoms of trouble with your plants and take preventative steps as needed, such as using organic pesticides or fungicides.

- Melons are harvested at different times depending on the type. Melons are ready to be picked when they reach their final color, emit their signature scent, and the stem linking it to the plant dries out and begins to fracture. For information on when to pick a particular variety, consult its care instructions.

If you follow these simple instructions, you can soon be harvesting your own juicy melons. Always remember to ask knowledgeable gardeners or study regional gardening guides for advice that will work in your area. Grow those melons with joy!

CHAPTER ONE
What Is The Point Of Cultivating Watermelons?

Growing melons may be a fun and profitable hobby for a number of reasons. The following are some strong arguments in favor of this idea:

• The opportunity to taste delicious, fresh fruit grown in your own garden is a major incentive for growing melons. The flavor and sweetness of melons produced at home often surpass that of commercially grown melons. It is a treat to gather a ripe melon and bite into its fragrant, luscious flesh.

• There is a great deal of variety in melons, both in terms of type and flavor. Try a variety of melons to find out one you like most; watermelons are refreshing, cantaloupes are sweet and aromatic, and honeydews have a subtle flavor. If you grow your own melons, you can experiment with rare heirloom kinds or new hybrid cultivars that you will not find in stores.

• Growing your own melons can be a money saver in the long run. During high demand times or if you opt for organic, the price of melons at the grocery store might skyrocket. The expense of buying melons can mount up quickly, but if you cultivate your own you can save money and never run out.

• Growing melons in your own yard gives you complete say over all aspects of their care and upkeep. If you and your family prefer to eat healthier, chemical-free fruits, you can choose to produce them organically, without the use of synthetic pesticides or fertilizers. To improve plant health and increase harvests, you can also try out various growth strategies, such as companion planting or trellising.

• Growing melons gives gardeners a chance to get in touch with nature and enjoy a satisfying gardening experience. It is possible to derive a lot of pleasure from cultivating a garden and reaping its rewards. Growing your own food can help you become a better gardener, increase your understanding of plant biology, and give you a new respect for the food you eat.

• Growing melons as a family or group project can be rewarding for everyone involved. Getting kids involved teaches them about farming, gives them a sense of ownership over their food, and makes for great memories. Sharing your melons with your neighbors and friends or selling them at a farmers market is a great way to meet new people and strengthen bonds within your community.

• Melons are beneficial to your health in more ways than one. They are low in fat and calories while being high in healthy vitamins like A and C and minerals like iron and potassium. Adding melons to your diet is a great way to improve your health and well-being.

Cultivating melons provides the pleasure of eating delicious, new fruit, financial savings, agency over growing methods, gardening fulfillment, family participation chances, and health benefits. It is satisfying to eat what you have grown, and it helps you develop a stronger bond with the food you eat.

Characteristics Of Various Melons

There is a huge range of melons, each with its own distinct flavor, texture, appearance, and even cultivation needs. Some common melons and their distinguishing features are listed below.

1. Citrullus lanatus (watermelon):

• There are many different kinds of watermelons to choose from, and some of the most popular include the

Crimson Sweet, Sugar Baby, Jubilee, and Charleston Gray.

• Characteristically, watermelons are extremely juicy and delicious due to their high water content. Fruits of all sizes, shapes, and colors are available, from little, spherical ones to enormous, elongated ones. Colors range from red to pink to yellow to orange for the flesh. The thick rind of a watermelon is often either striped or uniform green in color.

• Watermelons require hot, sunny weather and rich, well-drained soil to grow successfully. To flourish, vines need a lengthy growing season and lots of room to twine.

2. Cucumis melo (cantaloupe):

• In terms of cantaloupe types, Hale's Best, Ambrosia, Athena, and Sweet 'n Early are some of the most well-known and sought-after.

• Cantaloupes are distinguished by their sweet, aromatic flesh and distinctive musky scent. Some types contain green or yellow flesh, although orange is the most common. Cantaloupes are smaller than watermelons and feature a ribbed or netted skin.

• Cantaloupes need hot weather and lots of sunshine to grow well. They do best in consistently moist soil with good drainage. Some types can survive in cooler environments.

3. Cucumis melo, or honeydew:

• Honeydew melons come in a wide spectrum of colors and flavors, from green to orange to yellow flesh.

• Honeydews are characterized by their soft, pale green or yellow skin and their exceptionally delicious and juicy flesh. Depending on the cultivar, the flesh may be a light shade of green, orange, or yellow. Honeydews have a softer flavor than other melons like watermelons and cantaloupes.

• Honeydews are comparable to cantaloupes in terms of their growing requirements. They do best in sunny areas that do not get too cold. For fruits to mature to their full potential, a steady supply of water is crucial.

4. Cucumis melo, or muskmelon:

• Varieties: European cantaloupe, Galia, Charentais, and Crenshaw are all included among the muskmelons that make up the genus Muskmelon.

• Muskmelons are distinguished by their sweet, aromatic, and flavorful flesh. They come in a wide variety of sizes, forms, and hues. Both smooth and netted skin types exist, with a spectrum of flesh colors from orange to green. The rich flavor and sweet scent of muskmelons make them a popular fruit.

• To flourish, muskmelons need hot weather and lots of direct sunlight. Soil with good drainage and consistent watering is ideal. Some plant types are better suited to a certain weather pattern or geographical area.

There are many other types of melons besides the ones listed here. Consider your growing conditions, your particular taste preferences, and the unique qualities of each type of melon when making your selection.

You can get location-specific advice and suggestions from places like seed catalogs, agricultural extension offices, and local nurseries.

CHAPTER TWO
Instrumental Resources

You will need a few key pieces of equipment and tools to successfully cultivate melons. Some of the most important instruments and implements for growing melons are as follows:

• A garden spade or fork is necessary for turning the soil, digging planting holes, and mixing in soil supplements such as compost or organic matter.

• A garden hoe can be used to loosen the soil around your melon plants, allowing you to more easily pull weeds and fertilize your crop. Maintaining a friable, well-aerated soil structure is important for limiting weed growth and maximizing water uptake by plants.

• A little trowel or transplanting tool is useful for moving seedlings around and for planting melons with pinpoint accuracy. Small holes can be dug without uprooting the plant or damaging the roots.

• Melons need to be watered frequently, especially during dry months, so have a watering can or garden hose handy. To keep plants well hydrated, it is best to use a watering can or garden hose fitted with a spray nozzle.

• Mulch: Mulching around melon plants aids in controlling soil temperature, preventing the spread of weeds, and retaining soil moisture. Mulches are often made of organic materials like straw or wood chips.

• Some melons, especially vining forms like some watermelons, require a trellis or support structure to thrive. Fruits are less likely to rot when supported by trellises or fences, and you can use the vertical space they provide more efficiently.

• Pruning shears or secateurs can be used to trim away sick or dying branches, thin overgrown foliage, and control the spread of melon vines.

Pruning encourages healthy growth, lessens the likelihood of disease, and refocuses a plant's resources on yielding fruit.

• Plant supports: Melons are heavy fruits, therefore as they age, the branches supporting the melons may need reinforcement. Soft ties or tomato cages can be used to support vines that are packed with fruit without damaging the plant.

• The vines of melons can be secured to trellises or other support structures with the aid of garden twine or plant ties. As the plants expand, they keep the vines from swaying or snapping.

• Protect your hands from scrapes, blisters, and thorns when working with dirt, plants, and other garden items by wearing a robust pair of garden gloves.

To successfully cultivate melons, you will need these instruments and supplies. Tools and equipment for keeping a healthy and productive melon patch may be found, depending on your individual demands and gardening preferences.

Structure Of A Melon Plant

Better care and management of your melons will result from your familiarity with their anatomy. The main components of a melon plant are as follows:

• The melon plant's roots hold it firmly in place and draw moisture and nutrients up from the ground. They have a main taproot that extends downward vertically and lateral roots that branch out laterally. The growth and yield of a melon plant depend on its roots flourishing.

• The stem of a melon plant is the principal structural organ above ground, holding up the leaves, flowers, and fruit. It shoots up and out of the ground, developing limbs as it expands. The stem is the plant's central organ, responsible for distributing water, nutrients, and carbohydrates.

• Leaves: Usually green and palmate (hand-shaped) or lobed, the leaves of melon plants are very wide and broad. The leaves, which are held in place by petioles at the plant's stem, are where the photosynthesis process actually takes place. For optimal sugar synthesis and plant vitality, healthy leaves are crucial.

• Long, trailing stems called "runners" or "vines" are produced by several melons. Runner plants spread out horizontally across the ground, and some can even be trained to climb up trellises. Flowers and fruit develop from the side branches that they send out. To prevent the plant from growing too far and to ensure healthy fruit development, runners may need to be supported or pruned.

• Melon flowers are dioecious, meaning that the same plant can produce both male and female blooms. Male flowers often bloom earlier and in greater numbers. They produce pollen and have long, skinny stalks. Shortly after, the female flowers appear, and they are easily identifiable by the little swelling at their bases; this is the ovary, which, if pollinated, will eventually become the fruit.

• The fruit of the melon plant is prized for its culinary potential. It is the fruit that results when a female flower is pollinated. Depending on the type, melons can range in size, shape, color, and flavor. Shapes range from spherical to elongated, skins can be smooth or netted, and the flesh is often sweet and juicy.

• Tendrils are slender, coiling structures that develop from the axils of the leaves on melon plants. Plants' tendrils are crucial in their growth and stability because they allow the plant to climb or connect to supports.

Knowing the anatomy of a melon plant will allow you to evaluate its condition, spot problems, and provide the best care possible. A melon plant's output can be increased across the board if its roots, stem, leaves, blooms, and fruits are well cared for.

CHAPTER THREE
The Role Of Environmental Factors In The Development Of Melons

Melon plants' expansion and maturation are affected by a number of external variables. With this knowledge, you can provide the best possible environment for your melon plants to flourish. The growth and development of melons are affected by the following factors:

• Because they thrive best in the warm weather, melons need to be grown in a certain temperature range. Melon plants do best when the ambient air temperature is somewhere between 21 and 32 degrees Celsius. The opposite of rapid growth is a period of high heat, which can harm plants even under normal temperatures. Melon cultivars have different temperature tolerances, so it is important to pick ones that work in your area.

• Sunlight: Melons are sun-loving plants, so they need a lot of it to thrive. They require daily exposure to sunshine averaging between 6 and 8 hours. The growth, flowering, and fruiting of plants can all suffer from a lack of sunlight. Put your melon plants in a spot where they can bask in the sun all day long.

• Melon plants require rich, moist soil that drains well. The soil's pH should be between 6.0 and 7.0, and it should be friable, rich in organic matter, and somewhat acidic. Root rot is caused by the extra moisture that is retained in thick clay soils. The need for additives like compost or fertilizer to boost the soil's nutrient content and drainage can be ascertained by a soil test.

• Proper and steady irrigation is essential for melon plants, especially during the fruiting stage. Melons need consistent, thorough watering to maintain a consistently moist but not soggy soil environment.

Stunted growth, underdeveloped fruit, or cracking might arise from inconsistent hydration or drought stress. One to one and a half inches of water per week should be provided, with adjustments made for weather and the melon variety in question.

• The availability of certain nutrients is crucial for the healthy development and fruit set of melons. All of their nutritional needs, such as nitrogen, phosphorus, potassium, and micronutrients, are met. You can provide the plant with the nutrients it needs by doing a soil test to determine what nutrients are lacking or out of balance.

• Pollination is essential for the fruit development of melons. Cross-pollination, in which pollen is transported from a male flower to a female flower, is necessary for the production of most types of melons. Successful pollination and fruit set can be encouraged by maintaining a healthy population of pollinators in your garden, supplying adjacent flowering plants, and avoiding the use of chemicals toxic to bees.

• Aphids, cucumber beetles, powdery mildew, fungal infections, and bacterial diseases are just some of the pests and diseases that can attack melon plants. It is crucial to keep a close eye on your plants for any signs of pest damage or disease. The negative effects of pests and diseases on melon growth can be lessened by employing effective pest control techniques, such as the use of pesticides or disease-resistant genotypes.

By paying close attention to these characteristics and providing optimal circumstances for your melon plants, you may encourage their growth and development, resulting in robust foliage, profuse flowering, and a bountiful crop of tasty melons.

Melons: A Life History

From seed germination to harvest, melons go through a complex life cycle. The development of a melon can be roughly summarized as follows:

• Planting a melon seed in fertile soil initiates the life cycle. The seed will germinate if the conditions are right. After being exposed to water, the seed will enlarge, send out a little root (radicle) into the ground, and a shoot (plumule) towards the surface.

• The cotyledons, or first leaves, appear as the shoot emerges from the earth at the seedling stage. Until genuine leaves grow, the energy needs of the developing seedling are met by these leaves. The seedling keeps expanding its canopy of leaves and fortifying its foundation of roots.

• Once the seedling has taken root, it will undergo a period of vegetative development. The plant puts all of its energy into growing a strong root system and lush leaves. In this growth phase, the plant expands its stems and vines and produces many new leaves.

• When a melon plant reaches maturity, it goes through a metamorphosis known as flowering. Male and female blooms form on the same plant. Male flowers bloom first and generate pollen, whereas fertilized female flowers will grow into fruit from a tiny swelling at their bases called an ovary.

• Fruit growth in melons is dependent on pollination. Pollination is the process by which pollen is delivered from male to female flowers, typically by bees but also by other insects. Fertilization of the ovary, which happens when pollination is successful, causes fruit to form. A melon fruit forms from each female flower that is fertilized.

• Melon fruit is formed when a fertilized ovary grows and develops after being pollinated. The fruit develops from a tiny green fruit through several stages before reaching full maturity. The fruit becomes larger, changes color, and develops a new texture, flavor, and aroma.

• Melons go through a ripening process when they reach full maturity. The sweetness of the fruit increases, and its color deepens. When the fruit is mature, it gives off a nice scent. Melons have the highest flavor and quality when picked when they are at the peak of maturity.

• Melon harvesting occurs when the fruit has reached full ripeness. When to pick melons depends on the type of melon and how ripe you want it. The fruits may be underripe if picked too soon, or overripe and spoilt if picked too late.

• Seed Saving: Choose fully developed, delicious melons if you intend to save seeds for later planting. Take the time to clean and dry the seeds you have extracted from the fruit. Put the seeds away in a dry, cool spot for later.

• The life cycle of a melon plant ends with harvest or seed saving, when the plant enters a dormant period. The seeds can remain dormant until the next growth season if they are stored correctly. The seeds will germinate and start a new life cycle if the right parameters (moisture, temperature, and light) are satisfied.

The length of time spent in each stage of a melon's life cycle might change based on factors like the type of melon, how it is grown, and the weather. Knowing when to plant melons and how to care for them properly at each stage of development is greatly facilitated by familiarity with the plant's life cycle.

CHAPTER FOUR
How To Pick The Perfect Melon

Factors like as environment, gardening preferences, and desired melon qualities all play a role in making the decision of which melon variety to grow. Here are some important factors to think about when choosing a melon:

• When it comes to weather and climate, not all melons are created equal. Think about the average temperatures, humidity, and frost dates in your area. While some melons thrive in hotter climates, some do better in milder ones. To ensure the greatest possible yield, select a type that thrives in your local environment.

• Varieties of melons have different fruiting dates; some mature more quickly than others. Pay close attention to the information supplied on the "days to maturity" or "days to harvest" for each variety. This will give you a rough idea of how long it will take for the melons to ripen. Choose rapid-maturing types if your growing season is limited.

• Shape and Size of the Fruit: Melons range from small, personal-sized melons to enormous, elongated watermelons. Think about how you will be eating or using the melons.

Mini or tiny melon cultivars are a good option if you are short on room but still want to enjoy this summertime treat. Choose larger-sized fruit kinds if you intend to use them for serving purposes like slicing or sharing.

• Different types of melons have their own unique tastes and textures. While some melons are naturally sweet, others may have a more complex or interesting flavor. Think about if you want your melons sweet or if you would rather they had a sour edge. The flesh of some melons is crisp and crunchy, whereas that of others is softer and more juicy.

• Tolerance or resistance to diseases that commonly affect melons, like powdery mildew and fusarium wilt, is bred into some melon types. Choose disease-resistant types of melons if you have had problems with certain diseases in the past, and you will have healthier plants overall.

• Melons can be divided into two groups, self-pollinating (monoecious) and cross-pollinating (dioecious), based on their pollination needs. Self-pollinating cultivars do not need to be pollinated by other plants because they produce both male and female blooms on the same plant. Separate male and female plants, or neighboring suitable kinds, are required for cross-pollination. Before planting dioecious types, make sure you have adequate space and favorable weather for cross-pollination.

• Selection of melon types relies heavily on personal choice and, to a lesser extent, on experimentation. Think about the tastes, colors, and textures of the melon varieties that appeal to you the most. If you are looking for a way to spice up your gardening routine, try growing some unusual melons and see what you come up with.

You may learn about the many kinds of melons that are out there by consulting seed catalogs, visiting local nurseries, or reading gardening guides.

Pay close attention to the reviews, ratings, and suggestions made for each kind. It is also beneficial to network with local gardeners or agricultural extension services to learn about melons that thrive in your area.

Taking these into account will help you select melon varieties that will thrive in your garden and yield a tasty and pleasant crop.

Planting Seedling Watermelons

Growing your own melons from seeds is an enjoyable and economical hobby. The following is a detailed explanation of how to germinate melon seeds:

• Obtain your melon seeds from a reliable supplier, and make sure they are of a high grade. Choose a type that suits your tastes and growing conditions in terms of disease resistance, flavor, and other qualities.

• As warm-season crops, melons require precise timing. Plant seeds inside three to four weeks before the final frost in your area is predicted to occur. You can also straight sow the seeds outside when the soil has warmed and frost risk has passed if you have a long growth season.

• Melon seeds should be planted in prepared containers such as seed trays, peat pots, or miniature pots with drainage holes. Put some potting soil or seed starting mix into the pots.

• Making a shallow hollow in the soil, approximately an inch deep, is what you will use to plant the seeds. Put the holes about an inch or two apart. Cover the melon seeds with earth and plant two or three seeds in each hole. For optimal seed-to-soil contact, gently push the soil.

• After planting seeds in the soil, make sure to give it a good soaking. Keep the soil regularly moist without letting it become saturated. Avoid disturbing the seeds by watering gently or using a spray bottle.

• Melon seeds need a warm, bright environment in order to germinate. Set the containers near a sunny window or on a seedling heat pad heated to the proper level. If sunshine is scarce, provide artificial grow lights for 12-16 hours a day.

• The average germination time for melon seeds is 7-10 days, but this might range from variety to variety and from environment to environment. When the seeds germinate and the seedlings emerge, you should thin the crop to just one robust plant per planting hole.

• Once the seedlings have produced several sets of true leaves and the threat of frost has gone, they can be transplanted into larger containers or moved outdoors into the garden.

Over the course of a week, expose the seedlings to outdoor circumstances by progressively increasing the amount of time they spend in direct sunshine.

• When planting melons outside, it is best to do so in a sunny spot with well-drained soil. Plants should be spaced in accordance with the instructions made for their particular variety. Vine-bearing melons often require a sizable plot of land.

• Care and maintenance include continuous watering to keep the soil wet without becoming soaked. For better water retention, weed control, and temperature control in the soil, spread an organic mulch around your plants. Keep an eye out for pests, infections, and nutrient deficiency, and treat or prevent them as needed.

If you follow these instructions and give your melons plenty of care, you will have robust plants in no time that will provide excellent melons. Always remember to tailor your methods to the specific needs of the melon variety you end up working with.

CHAPTER FIVE
Watering Your Melon Plants

For optimal growth and yield, melon plants require special attention. Throughout the growing season, remember these essential care procedures:

• For optimal growth, melons need a steady supply of water. Be sure to saturate the soil all the way down to the plant's roots when you water them. Root rot and other fungal diseases can be caused by overwatering.

Aim for consistent soil moisture, especially during flowering and fruit set. To reduce the likelihood of fungal illnesses, it is best to water plants early in the day, when the air is cooler.

• To mulch, surround the stems of the melons with a layer of organic mulch like straw or compost. Mulching is useful for controlling soil temperature, preventing weed growth, and retaining moisture. It also serves as a barrier, stopping the melons from touching the ground and therefore lowering the likelihood of rotting.

• Fertilization is essential for melon growth and fruiting since melons are heavy feeders. Add compost or other organic debris that has had time to age before planting. In addition, use a slow-release granular fertilizer or a balanced organic fertilizer as directed. Compost or more fertilizer can be side-dressed as the plants grow to ensure a steady supply of nutrients.

• Trellises or other support structures are helpful for training and supporting vining melon varieties. You can conserve room, boost airflow, and decrease the likelihood of disease by teaching the vines to climb the supports.

Soft twine or plant ties should be used to gently secure the vines to the trellis. Straw or other supports may be necessary for bushier or sprawling kinds if you want to keep the fruits off the ground.

• Pruning melons increases airflow, lowers disease resistance, and shifts resources to fruit production. Remove any shoots or branches that are threatening the main stem by pinching them.

This triggers the plant to direct its resources toward fruit formation. Dead or diseased leaves or stems should be removed as soon as possible to stop the spread of infection.

• Pollination: Bees are the most important pollinators for melons. Planting bee-friendly flowers near your garden will entice pollinators to your yard. If you care about bees, you should not use pesticides. If you do not have enough bees or other pollinators, you can use a little paintbrush to move pollen from male to female melon blossoms.

• Management of Pests and Diseases: Be on the lookout for pests and illnesses on your melon plants regularly. Aphids, cucumber beetles, and squash bugs are common predators of melons.

Use natural approaches to pest management, such as manual removal, the application of soaps, oils, or other liquid insecticides, or the introduction of predatory insects like ladybugs or lacewings. Keep an eye out for powdery mildew and bacterial wilt, and respond accordingly by using fungicides or planting disease-resistant types.

• When picking melons, do so when they have reached their optimal ripeness and flavor. When a melon reaches maturity, it may alter color, aroma, or texture in a number of ways. The optimal time to harvest will vary according on the cultivar. Leave a short stem on the melon after harvesting it from the vine using a sharp knife or shears.

Following these guidelines will help ensure that your melon plants thrive, yield a lot of fruit, and are protected from pests and illnesses. Paying close attention to your melons on a regular basis will help you reap a bountiful harvest.

Facilitating Melon Development

It is important to provide adequate support for melons, especially vining kinds with long, trailing vines. By providing adequate support, you can increase airflow, lessen the likelihood of illness, facilitate harvesting, and free up valuable garden real estate. Some strategies for encouraging melon development are as follows:

• Space-saving and fruit-protecting, trellising melon vines is a common practice. Before the melons begin to climb, support them with robust trellises or wire mesh panels. Tenderly coax the vines into climbing the trellis or threading their way through the wire mesh as they expand.

The vines can be tied to the framework using either soft twine or plant ties. The developing melons will put a strain on the trellis, so make sure it is sturdy enough to support them.

• Melon vines can be supported by A-frame or teepee constructions erected from bamboo poles or wooden pegs. Construct an A-frame or teepee out of two or more poles, joining them at the top. You may start your own melon farm by planting seedlings at the foot of each structure and training the vines to climb up the poles as they grow. This procedure creates a strong framework against which the vines can ascend.

• Cages, often known as tomato cages, can be used to successfully sustain melon plants. Cage each melon plant extensively; the cage must be tall enough to support the climbing melons as they mature. Weave the melon vines carefully through the cage openings as they begin to grow. The melons are kept off the ground and the sprawling vines are contained by the cage.

• Supportive slings or hammocks can be used to carry heavier melons, such as larger watermelons. When the fruit begins to mature, hang a mesh hammock or soft fabric sling under the plants and fasten it to a strong support system. The melons are protected from rot and damage by being suspended in a sling or hammock off the ground.

• Individual stakes or poles can suffice as support for smaller melon varieties or in areas with limited space. Plant soft twine or plant ties near each melon plant and use these to attach the vines to the stakes as they grow. Using this technique, the vines are able to remain vertical rather than drooping to the floor.

It is important to remember to be gentle when supporting the melon vines and fruits so as not to harm the plant or cause the fruits to fall off prematurely.

Support the growing melons by checking and adjusting the supports as needed throughout the season. Melons benefit from a healthy environment that encourages their development and makes them easier to care for and harvest.

CHAPTER SIX
Yield Optimization For Melons

Here are some methods and suggestions for maximizing melon productivity and obtaining a plentiful harvest:

• Full sunlight is essential for the growth of melons. For optimal growth, melons need 6-8 hours of sunshine per day. Pick a spot that gets plenty of sunlight and stay away from any tall trees or buildings that could cast shadows on your garden.

• Give the melon plants room to expand and grow to their full potential. Even though bushier or more compact melon cultivars may not need as much room as their vining counterparts, they still require adequate space for air circulation. Avoid overpopulation and resource competition by giving your melons the space they need to thrive.

• Fertilizing and preparing the soil is essential before planting melon seedlings. To boost fertility, drainage, and water retention, amend the soil with organic matter like compost or well-aged manure. To ensure that your soil is suitable for producing melons, you should do a soil test to determine the nitrogen levels and pH.

• Mulching and Soil Moisture Management: To keep the soil

surrounding the melons moist, cover the ground with a layer of organic mulch, such as straw or wood chips. Mulch can be used to keep soil damp, moderate soil temperature, prevent weeds from sprouting, and cut down on water loss through evaporation. Regular watering, especially during dry spells, is necessary to keep the soil moist at a steady level. Root rot is caused by overwatering, so be careful.

• Support for Pollination: Bees are the most important pollinators for melons. Improve pollination by luring beneficial insects like bees to your yard with bee-friendly blooms, keeping bee-harming insecticides out of the picture, and giving bees a place to drink. If there are not enough bees or other pollinators around, you can use a small brush to move pollen from male to female melon blossoms.

• Pruning and training: Melons benefit from selective pruning to increase air circulation and decrease susceptibility to fungal diseases. Remove any shoots or branches that are threatening the main stem by pinching them. In order to maximize efficiency and minimize waste of space, vines should be trained along trellises, cages, or other support systems. This prevents the fruit from touching the ground and spoiling.

• Fertilization is essential for melon growth and fruiting since melons are heavy feeders. Soil fertility can be improved by adding organic matter before to planting. In addition, use a balanced fertilizer or a melon-specific fertilizer and apply it as directed. Apply compost or supplemental fertilizer as a side-dressing to the plants periodically throughout the growth season.

• Management of Pests and Diseases: Be on the lookout for pests and illnesses on your melon plants regularly. Check for insect damage, as well as the symptoms of any diseases, on the plant's leaves, stems, and fruits.

Use natural approaches to pest management, such as manual removal, the application of soaps, oils, or other liquid insecticides, or the introduction of predatory insects. Maintaining proper garden hygiene necessitates the quick removal of any infected plant material.

• Melons are at their most delicious and sweetest when they are picked at their peak ripeness. Color, smell, and texture changes are only few of the indicators of ripeness for melons. For the best harvest results, follow the advice given for your particular variety. The best-tasting melons can only be had if they are harvested at the optimal moment.

You may increase the production of your melon plants and enjoy a bountiful crop of tasty and juicy melons by following these steps and caring for your plants properly during the growing season.

Melons: Gathering And Keeping Them

If you want the maximum flavor and quality from your melons, you need to harvest them at the right time and store them correctly. Here are some tips on how to pick melons and keep them fresh:

1. Time of Harvesting: Mature melons show varying characteristics depending on the variety. The following are some broad signs of trouble:

• The skin color of the melon should mature and change as it ripens. Watermelons, for instance, might show their readiness for consumption by developing a dull skin tone or a yellow patch on the underside.

• Rather than a dull thud, a ripe melon should make a deep, hollow sound when tapped. Watermelons and other large melons benefit greatly from this strategy.

• Scent: ripe melons typically have a nice, sugary scent. The stem end of the melon should give off a distinct aroma when it is ready to be picked.

• A mature melon's skin will feel firm without being excessively tough. When gently pressed, it should give just a little.

2. Melons can be harvested by cutting them from the vine with a sharp knife or shears and leaving a small piece of the stem connected to the fruit. Do not twist or tug on the melon, as this could cause harm to the vine or the actual melon itself. Take care not to bruise the melons when you handle them.

3. After picking melons, be careful not to bruise or otherwise damage their skin by handling them roughly. Put the melons in a clean, well-padded basket or other storage container.

It is best not to stack the melons on top of each other, as this could cause the fruits on the bottom to get bruised or crushed.

4. Some melons, like cantaloupes, taste better after being picked early and allowed to mature somewhat off the vine. When storing harvested melons, it is best to do it at room temperature in a warm, well-ventilated place.

This lets their natural sweetness and flavor come out to play. Watermelons and other types of melons, however, do not continue to mature once they have been picked.

5. Melons should be eaten soon after harvest because their flavor improves with time. Here are some recommendations for the brief storage of melons:

• Melons will last longer if stored between 45 and 50 degrees Fahrenheit (7 and 10 degrees Celsius). However, some melons, such as watermelons, lose flavor and texture when refrigerated, so it is better to eat them as soon as possible.

• Melons thrive in environments with low to medium humidity. Mold and spoiling can occur at high humidity levels, while dehydration can occur at low humidity levels. Maintain a relative humidity in the range of 75–85 percent.

• Keep melons in a cool, dry place, apart from other fruits and vegetables, and in their own storage area. The ethylene gas given off by melons has been shown to hasten the ripening of surrounding fruit and vegetables.

• Do not wash melons until right before eating them to preserve their flavor. Surface moisture can promote the growth of mold and rot.

Keep in mind that the recommended storage length for melons is short in comparison to other fruits, so enjoy them as soon as possible after harvest.

CHAPTER SEVEN
Common Difficulties And Solutions

There are some difficulties that can arise when growing melons. If you are trying to cultivate melons, you should be aware of the following issues and solutions:

1. Infestations of Pests:

• Melon plants may be plagued by aphids, cucumber beetles, squash bugs, and spider mites, among other pests.

• Handpicking, the use of insecticidal soaps or oils, and the introduction of beneficial insects like ladybugs and lacewings are all examples of organic pest management approaches. Keep an eye out for any telltale signs of pest damage to your plants, and respond quickly if you see any.

2. Infectious Disease:

• Powdery mildew, downy mildew, and fusarium wilt are just a few of the fungal diseases that can attack melon plants.

• Good garden hygiene requires the prompt removal and proper disposal of any infected plant parts. Avoid encouraging fungal illnesses by watering from above and making sure plants have enough room to breathe. As a preventative measure, or as instructed by a local gardening expert, you may choose to plant disease-resistant melon types and use organic fungicides or bactericides.

3. Failure to Set Fruit or Fruit Size:

• Issue: Poor fruit set or tiny fruits might result from insufficient pollination, high temperatures, nutrient deficits, or inappropriate watering.

• Planting bee-friendly flowers in the area and avoiding the use of chemicals that can be harmful to bees are two solutions to this problem. Always make sure your melon plants have plenty of water, sunlight, and fertilizer. In order to ensure the plants have all the nutrients they need to produce healthy fruit, you need fertilize them on a regular basis with a balanced organic fertilizer.

4. Fruits that are too ripe or too unripe:

• The flavor and texture of melons might be negatively impacted if they are picked too early or too late, respectively.

• The solution is to learn the telltale signs of ripeness for each type of melon. Keep an eye out for variations in hue, volume, sound, scent, and texture. Picking melons when they are at their tastiest and sweetest is essential.

5. Subpar flavor or quality of the fruit:

• Issue: Lack of sunlight, high or low temperatures, poor watering, and nutrient imbalances are just some of the environmental issues that can negatively affect fruit quality and flavor.

• Full sunlight, regular watering, and sufficient nutrients are essential for healthy melon plant growth, thus this problem can be solved. Before planting, enrich the soil with organic materials to make it well-drained and fertile. Check for nutritional inadequacies by performing a soil test, and then make the necessary adjustments.

6. Space Restriction and Vine Control:

• The problem with growing vining melons is that they can quickly take over a garden if not contained.

• Trellising, cages, or other support structures can be used to train the vines and make better use of the available area. Remove any competing shoots or branches from the plant's periphery on a regular basis. Overcrowding can be prevented or at least reduced with careful planting spacing.

• You can have a more fruitful growth season and a better harvest if you take the time to anticipate and resolve these frequent problems that affect melon plants.

Superior Methods For Growing Melons

Experienced gardeners can benefit from learning cutting-edge methods for cultivating melons. The following are some cutting-edge methods to consider:

• Melon plants benefit from a regulated atmosphere, an extended growing season, and protection from inclement weather when grown in a high tunnel or greenhouse. Increased yields and earlier harvests are both possible because to the climate control provided by these structures. In addition, they safeguard the melon crop from harmful organisms, leading to higher yields.

• Hydroponics and aquaponics are soil-less growing methods that can be used to grow melons. In this method, melon plants get everything they need from a nutrient-rich water solution or, in the case of aquaponics, from fish excrement. Growth may be maximized and yields can be boosted by using hydroponics or aquaponics because of the increased control over nutrient supply, water availability, and environmental conditions.

• Melons can be grown vertically, making better use of available space, with the help of vertical gardening techniques. Melons can be grown on trellises, in containers hung on walls, or in hanging baskets. This technique works great for dwarf or shrub types. The vines need to be trained and pruned regularly so that they grow upward and do not get too crowded.

• Closer plant spacing is used in intensive planting of melons to increase yield. Growing more melons in the same space is possible if you prune back the distance between each

to Extend the Growing Season: Row covers, cold frames, and frost blankets are just some of the methods that can be used to protect melons from frost and lower plant. Overcrowding and disease can be avoided by keeping an eye on the plants and making sure they have enough food, water, and ventilation.

• Melon plants can be better controlled by employing sophisticated trimming procedures. To promote the development of the main stems and to channel the plant's energy into fruit production, it is common practice to pinch off lateral shoots, commonly known as suckers.

In addition, you can improve airflow and decrease the likelihood of illnesses like powdery mildew by performing some selective pruning to remove dead or diseased branches and leaves.

• The scion of one attractive melon type is grafted onto the rootstock of another melon or cucumber plant during the grafting process. When done correctly, grafting can strengthen a plant's immune system, boost its vitality, and boost its productivity. Growers can now cultivate watermelons that are less susceptible to certain diseases and environmental factors.

• Methods temperatures and so extend the growing season. These buildings produce a microclimate that acts as insulation and keeps in warm air. These coverings are ideal for planting early-season melons so that they can be harvested sooner.

• If natural pollination is difficult, you can try employing advanced pollination techniques, such as hand pollination or vibrating flowers with an electric toothbrush to spread pollen. In locations where there are few pollinators or where pollinator activity is minimal, these techniques can be invaluable.

Keep in mind that sophisticated methods of melon cultivation call for close observation, meticulous care, and experience.

Before putting a method into practice, it is crucial to learn all you can about it and meet whatever prerequisites it has. Exciting new developments and increased melon yields can be achieved through experimentation and the adaptation of procedures to your unique growing conditions.

CHAPTER EIGHT
Have Fun With Your Melons

You have worked hard to cultivate and gather your melons, and now you can reward yourself with their sweet flavor. Here are some ways to enjoy your melons to their fullest:

• Consumption in its fresh state is the best and simplest way to enjoy melons. Enjoy the delicious, juicy flesh of the melon by slicing it into wedges or cubes. Refreshing on a hot day, it is best served cold. Melon is a versatile fruit that may be added to a fruit salad or used as a garnish for other foods like yogurt, pancakes, or desserts.

• Refreshing melon smoothies and juices can be made by blending ripe melon with ice and a dash of lime juice. Melon can be combined with other fruits or given an extra kick from mint or ginger. You can enjoy the juice of melons on its own or in a blend with other fruit juices by using a juicer to extract the juice.

• Sorbets and granitas made from melons are a refreshing way to end a meal. Melon sorbet is prepared by pureeing the melon flesh, to which optional sugar or honey is added, and then freezing the resulting concoction in an ice cream machine. You can also make a mushy melon granita by simply freezing the puree in a shallow pan and scraping it with a fork every hour.

• Delicious melon salads can be made by combining the fruit with other raw, fresh ingredients. Melon goes well with salty and sour toppings like feta cheese, prosciutto, mint, and arugula. For added taste, try drizzling with a little citrus juice or balsamic vinegar.

• Make some unique melon salsa or chutney in the kitchen and show off your culinary flair. You can make a tasty salsa by chopping up some melon and mixing it with other ingredients like onions, jalapenos, cilantro, lime juice, and spices.

Alternately, melon can be made into a delicious chutney by simmering it with vinegar, sugar, and spices; it goes great with grilled meats or cheese.

• Try out some new sweets where melons are the main attraction. Freeze the blended melon with either water or juice in popsicle molds for a refreshing summer treat. Make a statement with desserts that feature melons, such as melon panna cotta, melon tarts, or cakes and muffins made with melons.

• If you find yourself with an abundance of melons, you might want to try your hand at creating some melon preserves. Canning melons into jams, jellies, or fruit preserves locks in their natural sugars and sweetness. When the growing season is gone, you can still enjoy the delicious flavors of melons.

Keep in mind that melons are at their most flavorful when they are fully ripe and at their freshest. If you want to enjoy the freshest flavor possible from your melons, eat them as soon as possible after harvesting.

Melon is finest when shared with others, so make sure to share your harvest. Melons have their own distinct flavors and textures, so do not be afraid to get creative in the kitchen and try new things.

Fixing The Most Frequent Watermelon Growing Issues

There are a number of potential problems that might impair the health and yield of your melons. Here are some frequent issues with producing melons and some solutions to them:

1. Mildew Powder:

• Melon plants are susceptible to a fungal disease known as powdery mildew, which manifests as a white powdery covering on the plant's leaves, stems, and fruits.

• Improving ventilation can be as simple as rearranging plant placement or cutting back overgrown shrubbery. Keep the leaves dry by watering the soil rather than the plant itself. Powdery mildew can be managed with the use of organic fungicides or a DIY treatment, such as a milk and water mixture. Choose melons that are more likely to resist pests and illnesses.

2. Flower Decay:

• Sunken, black, and leathery areas at the blossom end of the fruit are symptoms of blossom end rot. It is brought on by either a lack of calcium or erratic water content.

• The problem can be fixed by regularly and deeply watering melon plants, so that the soil is always moist. Apply mulch around plants to keep soil moist. Keep the soil at a healthy pH and fertility level to maximize calcium absorption. Think about employing foliar sprays or amending the soil with calcium.

3. Pollination Failure and Low Fruit Bearing:

• Inadequate pollination can cause low yields or unattractive fruit shapes.

• Planting flowers that bees and butterflies enjoy in the area is one possible solution. Pollen is transferred from male to female melons by hand using a tiny brush or cotton swab. To facilitate pollen release and transport, gently vibrate the blossoms with an electric toothbrush.

4. Infestations of Pests:

• Issue Aphids, cucumber beetles, squash bugs, and spider mites are just some of the pests that can attack melon plants.

• Use natural techniques of pest management, such as the use of insecticidal soaps or oils, the release of beneficial insects like ladybugs and lacewings, and the cultivation of pest-repellent companion plants. It is important to keep a close eye on your plants and respond quickly if you notice any symptoms of pest activity.

5. Cracking Fruit:

• Melons' skins are prone to cracking, especially after a lot of rain or if you do not water them consistently.

• Resolve: Water melons thoroughly but infrequently such that the soil is always slightly damp but never soggy. Put down mulch around your plants to keep the soil nice and moist. To avoid overripening and possible cracking, melons should be harvested as soon as they reach maturity.

6. Smaller than Average Fruit:

• Poor pollination, insufficient nutrients, or environmental stress could all contribute to undersized melon fruits, which is a problem.

• Solution: Promote pollinators and, if necessary, employ hand-pollination methods to ensure adequate pollination. Provide well-balanced organic fertilizers and soil amendments like compost to keep soil fertility at an optimum level. Be sure to give your plants enough of room to develop, water, and sunlight.

7. Leaves Turning Yellow:

• Leaves that have become yellow may be a symptom of overwatering, nutrient shortages, or a disease.

• Conduct a soil test to determine what nutrients are missing, and then provide them. Make required changes to drainage and watering schedules to avoid overwatering. Good garden hygiene, the use of organic fungicides or bactericides, or consulting a local gardening expert are all effective ways to combat underlying disease problems.

Keep in mind that prevention is the key to sustaining robust melon crops.

Common melon growing issues can be mitigated with careful attention to detail, consistent monitoring, and prompt action.

Conclusion

Growing melons is a fun and potentially lucrative hobby. You can provide the best possible conditions for your melon plants by learning about their anatomy, life cycle, and the elements that affect their growth and development. Depending on your growth conditions, available area, and personal tastes, you will want to select a melon variety carefully.

Growing melons from seed gives you complete command over the process.

Plant health and fruit production can be optimized with regular attention to watering, fertilizing, and controlling pests. Space can be conserved and airflow improved by providing vertical support for growing melons.

Providing ideal growing conditions and being proactive in the face of frequent problems are essential to achieving maximum melon production. Melons lose their flavor and quality if you do not pick them when they are ripe and put them in the fridge right away.

High tunnel farming, hydroponics, and vertical gardening are all cutting-edge methods that seasoned gardeners can use to take their melons to the next level.

The growing season can be prolonged and productivity increased by using modern pollination techniques, intensive planting, and season extension strategies.

At last, when your melon crop is mature, you can eat it. Enjoy the sweet and juicy flavors of melons whether you consume them fresh, incorporate them into different recipes, or store them for later use.

Keep in mind that every season is a chance to get better at growing melons. Growing your own luscious melons from seed requires patience, observation, and flexibility, but the rewards are worth it.

THE END

110

Made in the USA
Monee, IL
23 June 2024

60380230R00066